ADVENT
He is Coming

BRUCE DOWNES

Advent Daily Devotional
© 2025 by Bruce Downes
ISBN: 979-8-9935368-2-8

For more information, contact:

Bruce Downes Ministries
PO Box 55750
Phoenix, AZ 85078
(602) 612-9705
BruceDownes.org

Unless otherwise noted, Scripture quotations are from the NEW REVISED STANDARD VERSION. Copyright © 1989, Division of Christian Education of the National Council of Churches of Christ in the U.S.A. Used by permission. All rights reserved.

CONTENTS PAGE

INTRODUCTION   5

WEEK 1 - THE PROMISE OF HIS COMING   9

Day 1   The Waiting Heart   11

Day 2   God's Perfect Timing   13

Day 3   The Faithful Promise   15

Day 4   The God Who Sees   17

Day 5   Hope that does not Disappoint   19

Day 6   Strength in the Waiting   21

Day 7   Light in the Darkness   23

WEEK 2 – PREPARE THE WAY   25

Day 8   A Voice in the Wilderness   27

Day 9   The Gift of Repentance   29

Day 10   A Clean Heart   31

Day 11   Turning Toward the Light   33

Day 12   The Peace of Surrender   35

Day 13   The Courage to Change   37

Day 14   A Heart that Listens   39

HE IS COMING ADVENT DEVOTIONAL

WEEK 3 – REJOICE, HE IS NEAR   41

    Day 15   The Path of Peace   43

    Day 16   The Joy of His Nearness   45

    Day 17   Joy in the Ordinary   47

    Day 18   The Joy of Giving   49

    Day 19   Joy that Strengthens   51

    Day 20   Joy in Believing   53

    Day 21   Emmanuel, God with Us   55

WEEK 4 – HE IS HERE   57

    Day 22   The Presence that Brings Peace   59

    Day 23   The Light of the World   61

    Day 24   The Humble King   63

    Day 25   The God Who Comes Close   65

CHRISTMAS DAY   69

WHAT'S NEXT?   71

INTRODUCTION

Advent is a sacred time of waiting, not an empty waiting, but one filled with promise, preparation, and hope. It is the season when we turn our hearts toward the coming of Jesus, remembering that He has come, that He still comes to us now, and that He will come again. Each year, the Church invites us to enter this season not as a routine but as a renewal, a chance to make room again for the presence of God in our everyday lives.

This devotional helps you walk that journey one day at a time. Over these twenty-six days, you will slow down, pray, and listen for the gentle voice of the Lord. Each day includes Scripture from the NRSV Bible, a short reflection to meditate on, a prayer, and journal prompts designed to help you integrate the message into your daily life. These moments of prayer and reflection do not add to your schedule but create sacred pauses and moments of encounter with the God who draws near.

The theme of this devotional, *He Is Coming*, reminds us that the message of Advent extends beyond the past or the future; it speaks truth for the present. God comes to you today. He enters your circumstances, your home, your heart. As you journey through these weeks of promise, preparation, and joy, may your waiting become worship and your hope grow into faith. And when Christmas morning arrives, may you know more deeply than ever before that Christ has come, and that He walks with you still.

HOW TO USE THIS DEVOTIONAL

This devotional follows the traditional four-week structure of Advent, beginning the fourth Sunday before Christmas. Here's how to make the most of your journey:

DAILY STRUCTURE

Each day includes four elements designed to guide your reflection:

1. **Scripture** - A passage from the NRSV Bible that anchors the day's theme. Read it slowly, perhaps more than once. Let the words settle in your heart before moving to the reflection.

2. **Devotional Reflection** - A meditation connecting the Scripture to the Advent themes and to your daily life. Don't rush through this. If a sentence speaks to you, pause and let God speak through it.

3. **Journal Prompts** - Two questions to help you personalize the message. The first directs you inward to your own spiritual life. The second calls you outward to consider how you might live as an IMPACTER - someone whose life reflects Christ's presence to others. You don't need to write lengthy responses; even a few honest sentences can be powerful.

4. **Prayer** - A prayer to guide your conversation with God. You can pray these words exactly as written or use them as a starting point for your own prayers.

WEEKLY RHYTHM

The devotional is organized into four weeks, each with its own theme:

- ○ Week 1: The Promise of His Coming - Awakening hope
- ○ Week 2: Prepare the Way - Renewing the heart
- ○ Week 3: Rejoice, He Is Near - Celebrating His presence
- ○ Week 4: He Is Here - Living in His light

Each week begins with an introduction to help you orient yourself to the theme. Read this at the start of the week to help you understand where the journey is leading.

FLEXIBILITY AND GRACE

If you miss a day, don't let guilt keep you from returning. Simply pick up where you left off. This devotional serves you; you don't serve it. On some days, you may spend thirty minutes in deep reflection. On other days, five minutes with Scripture and prayer may be all you can manage. God meets you in both.

BECOMING IMPACTERS

Throughout this devotional, you will encounter the term IMPACTER in the journal prompts. An IMPACTER is someone whose encounter with Christ compels them to make an impact in the world around them. It is not about grand gestures but about letting Christ's light, love, and presence overflow from your life into your everyday relationships and circumstances. As you reflect on becoming an IMPACTER, think about specific people, situations, and opportunities where God might be calling you to be His hands, feet, and heart.

MOVING BEYOND ADVENT

While this devotional focuses on the Advent season, its goal is to establish rhythms of prayer, Scripture reading, and reflection that continue long after Christmas. May these twenty-six days become a doorway into a deeper walk with God that carries you through the entire year.

Now, take a deep breath. Light a candle if you wish. Turn off distractions. Open your heart.

The Lord is near, and He is waiting to meet you here.

A Week to Awaken Hope

THE PROMISE OF HIS COMING

Advent begins with promise.

God's voice gently stirs, calling His people to remember that He keeps every word He speaks. Before the first Christmas night, the prophets carried God's promise through generations of waiting: light would dawn and the Savior would come. In the same way, we too lift our eyes beyond what feels delayed or uncertain and fix them on the One who never fails to keep His word.

This week awakens hope. We dare to believe again that God's timing is perfect and His plans are sure. We look at our world, our families and our hearts, trusting that the same God who fulfilled His promise in Bethlehem will also fulfill His promises in us. When we fill waiting with faith, we do not waste it. The Lord draws near, and He works in ways unseen.

THIS WEEK'S JOURNEY

- o Day 1: The Waiting Heart - Learning to wait with trust
- o Day 2: God's Perfect Timing - Surrendering our schedules to His
- o Day 3: The Faithful Promise - Remembering God's unchanging character

9

- o Day 4: The God Who Sees - Knowing we are not forgotten
- o Day 5: Hope That Does Not Disappoint - Anchoring in God's love
- o Day 6: Strength in the Waiting - Finding renewal in surrender
- o Day 7: Light in the Darkness - Recognizing Christ's presence now

PRAYER FOR THE WEEK

Come, Lord Jesus.
Let hope rise where it has faded,
Let faith renew where it has grown weary
and let every longing heart find certainty in You.
We wait for You with expectant hearts.
Father, we ask this in Jesus' name,
through the power of the Holy Spirit.
Amen.

DAY 1

THE WAITING HEART

"I wait for the Lord, my soul waits, and in his word I hope." Psalm 130:5

DEVOTIONAL REFLECTION

Advent begins with waiting.

Not the restless kind that checks the clock every few minutes. Not the anxious kind that fears what might never come. This waiting invites us to slow down and make space for God's presence. In a world that moves quickly and demands instant results, such waiting can feel uncomfortable. Yet Scripture teaches us to wait on the Lord as a holy act of trust. In the stillness, we begin to hear His voice and sense His quiet work within us.

The people of Israel waited for centuries for the coming of the Messiah. They did not waste their waiting because God prepared hearts and wove His plan of redemption through history. In the same way, the Lord works in the hidden places of our lives, even when nothing seems to change. Waiting teaches us to depend on His faithfulness rather than our own control.

As we begin this Advent journey, let your heart rest in the knowledge that God draws near. Each moment of waiting prepares a space where grace can take root. The Lord has not forgotten you. His word stands true, His promises remain certain, and His love already comes to you.

JOURNAL PROMPTS

1. Think of one specific situation in your life right now where you're waiting for God to act. What would it look like to wait with trust instead of anxiety in that situation this week?

2. Who in your circle of friends, family, or coworkers is struggling to believe that God sees their waiting? How might you encourage them this week and become an IMPACTER of hope?

PRAYER

Loving Father,
Help me wait with faith and peace in my heart.
Teach me to rest in Your timing
and trust in Your promises.
When impatience rises,
remind me that You work
even when I cannot see.
Fill my heart with quiet hope
as I prepare for the coming of Jesus.
Let my waiting become worship,
and my longing become love.
Father, I ask this in Jesus' name,
through the power of the Holy Spirit.
Amen.

DAY 2

GOD'S PERFECT TIMING

"But when the fullness of time had come, God sent his Son, born of a woman, born under the law."
Galatians 4:4

DEVOTIONAL REFLECTION

God is never late.

Every part of His plan unfolds in perfect timing, even when it feels delayed from our perspective. For generations, the people of Israel longed for the Messiah, praying for freedom and restoration. The centuries felt endless, yet when the moment came, God sent His Son into the world. Every promise, every prophecy, every longing heart found fulfillment in Jesus Christ.

Waiting often stretches our faith, especially when we cannot understand what God does. We mistake His silence for absence when He actually prepares everything for the fullness of time. We must remain faithful and open, trusting that He completes His plans with wisdom beyond our sight.

When we surrender our timing to God's timing, peace grows. Advent reminds us that God's delays do not mean denial, and that His purposes always come to pass. The same Lord who fulfilled His promise in Bethlehem will fulfill His promises in you. Rest in His perfect timing and let your heart find joy in knowing that He is always at work.

JOURNAL PROMPTS

1. Name one specific area where you've struggled to trust God's timing in the past year. What did that struggle teach you about your relationship with Him?

2. Think of someone who feels discouraged by delayed answers to prayer. What encouragement from your own experience of God's timing could you share with them this week?

PRAYER

Lord Jesus,
Help me to trust in the rhythm of Your timing.
When I am tempted to rush ahead,
teach me to rest in Your wisdom and Your love.
Let patience grow in me
as I wait for Your promises to unfold.
Fill me with peace that comes from
knowing You are in control of all things.
In this Advent season,
I surrender my schedule to Yours.
Father, I ask this in Jesus' name,
through the power of the Holy Spirit.
Amen.

DAY 3

THE FAITHFUL PROMISE

---

*"Know therefore that the Lord your God is God,
the faithful God who maintains covenant loyalty
with those who love him and keep his
commandments, to a thousand generations."*
Deuteronomy 7:9

DEVOTIONAL REFLECTION

God's promises stand unshakable because His character
never changes.

From the beginning of time, He has bound Himself to His
people with steadfast love. He roots every covenant He
makes in His faithfulness, not in our perfection. Even when
humanity wanders, God continues to draw His children
back, keeping His word through mercy and compassion.

When we reflect on the birth of Jesus, we see the ultimate
fulfillment of God's promise. Centuries of waiting found
their answer in a manger, where the eternal Word became
flesh and lived among us. This story reaches beyond the
past; it stands as a living reminder that God always does
what He says He will do.

Sometimes our hearts doubt that faithfulness when prayers
seem unanswered. However, Advent invites us to remember
that God's timing and faithfulness work together as one. He

proves faithful today, as He was to Abraham, to David, and to Mary. When we hold on to His promises, hope takes root again.

JOURNAL PROMPTS

1. List three specific ways you've seen God's faithfulness in your life over the past five years. How do these memories strengthen your trust in Him today?

2. Who needs to hear a story of God's faithfulness from you this week? Plan when and how you'll share it to become an IMPACTER of faith.

PRAYER

Faithful God,
You are constant and true in all Your ways.
Thank You for keeping Your promises
and for never forgetting Your people.
Strengthen my faith when I grow weary in waiting.
Help me remember the ways
You have already shown Your goodness to me.
May I walk in trust and gratitude,
knowing that Your covenant love endures forever.
Father, I ask this in Jesus' name,
through the power of the Holy Spirit.
Amen.

DAY 4

THE GOD WHO SEES

"So she named the Lord who spoke to her, 'You are El-roi'; for she said, 'Have I really seen God and remained alive after seeing him?'" Genesis 16:13

DEVOTIONAL REFLECTION

Long before shepherds saw the glory of God in the night sky, a woman named Hagar discovered that God saw her.

In the wilderness, far from home and uncertain of her future, she encountered the Lord who knew her by name. She called Him El-roi, "the God who sees." That same God still sees each of us today.

Hagar's wilderness experience mirrors the long wait of God's people during Advent. Like Israel in exile, like the faithful who longed for the Messiah, Hagar waited in a barren place, wondering if God remembered His promises. Yet in that very wilderness, God met her. He saw her tears, heard her fears, and promised that her story was not over. This is the pattern of Advent: God sees us precisely in the places where we feel most forgotten.

When we realize that God sees us, hope is born again. Our Advent waiting turns sacred because we know that He notices every moment, every prayer, every hidden longing of the heart. The same God who met Hagar in the wilderness

17

and came to shepherds in the night also comes to you today, seeing your needs, your questions, and your love.

JOURNAL PROMPTS

1. Where in your life right now do you feel like Hagar—forgotten, in the wilderness, wondering if God sees you? Be specific about the situation.

2. Who around you feels invisible or overlooked? Name one concrete action you'll take this week to show them they are seen, becoming an IMPACTER of His compassionate gaze.

PRAYER

El-roi, the God who sees,
Thank You for seeing me just as I am.
In my wilderness seasons,
when I wonder if You remember Your promises,
meet me as You met Hagar.
When I feel unseen or forgotten,
remind me that I am always before Your eyes.
Let Your gaze heal the places in me
that hide in fear.
As I wait this Advent,
help me trust that You see,
You know, and You are coming.
Father, I ask this in Jesus' name,
through the power of the Holy Spirit.
Amen.

DAY 5

HOPE THAT DOES NOT DISAPPOINT

"And hope does not disappoint us, because God's love has been poured into our hearts through the Holy Spirit that has been given to us." Romans 5:5

DEVOTIONAL REFLECTION

Sometimes hope feels fragile.

Waiting seems endless. Answers appear far away. Yet Scripture tells us that true hope in God will never disappoint. It differs from wishful thinking or vague optimism; it offers deep assurance that God's love will have the final word.

Advent plants this kind of hope again. We remember that the world waited in darkness until Christ came, and His light has never gone out. The hope we carry finds its ground in the reality of God's love poured into our hearts through the Holy Spirit. Even when circumstances shift, His presence remains constant, and His promises remain sure.

God's love is not just a feeling; it lives as a power that sustains us. Every time we open our hearts in prayer, we give hope a place to grow. As we look toward Christmas, let that hope rise again, not because everything is perfect, but

19

because the One who is perfect has already come and continues coming still.

JOURNAL PROMPTS

1. Name three specific situations in your life right now that need God's hope instead of your fear or discouragement. What would change if you truly believed hope would not disappoint?

2. Think of someone who has lost hope recently - perhaps facing illness, job loss, or relational pain. What specific words or actions could you offer them this week as an IMPACTER of Christ's unwavering love?

PRAYER

God of hope,
Fill my heart again with Your steadfast love.
When I am weary or uncertain,
remind me that my hope in You will never be wasted.
Let Your Spirit renew my confidence
and strengthen my faith.
Help me to hold fast to the promises You have spoken,
and to share that same hope with others who need it most.
Father, I ask this in Jesus' name,
through the power of the Holy Spirit.
Amen.

DAY 6

STRENGTH IN THE WAITING

"But those who wait for the Lord shall renew their strength, they shall mount up with wings like eagles, they shall run and not be weary, they shall walk and not faint." Isaiah 40:31

DEVOTIONAL REFLECTION

Waiting feels like standing still while everything around us moves forward.

Yet in heaven's eyes, waiting is not inactivity; it is strength in the making. Scripture assures us that those who wait on the Lord will find new energy and endurance. The promise is not that the waiting will be short, but that we will not face it alone.

In Advent, we learn again that strength does not come from striving but from surrender. The Lord renews us as we lean into His presence, trusting that His plan unfolds even when we cannot see it. Like an eagle that soars higher on unseen wind, the Spirit lifts us when we rest our hope in Him.

The one who waits on God discovers that strength comes not from control but from communion. As you wait for God to move in your life, trust that He already works in ways beyond your sight. He will give you the grace to walk, to run, and to rise.

21

JOURNAL PROMPTS

1. In what specific area of your life are you trying to manufacture strength through your own effort rather than waiting on God? What would surrendering that area look like this week?

2. Who in your life is exhausted and running on empty? How could you be an IMPACTER tangibly strengthening them this week, perhaps through a meal, a listening ear, or practical help or encouragement?

PRAYER

Lord,
When my strength fades,
lift me up by the power of Your Spirit.
Help me to wait on You with courage and patience.
Renew my heart so that
I may walk in Your peace and not grow weary.
Thank You that in my weakness, You are my strength.
May my waiting become a witness of Your faithfulness.
Father, I ask this in Jesus' name,
through the power of the Holy Spirit.
Amen.

DAY 7

LIGHT IN THE DARKNESS

"The light shines in the darkness, and the darkness did not overcome it." John 1:5

DEVOTIONAL REFLECTION

Before the birth of Jesus, the world waited in darkness.

The prophets spoke of light to come, and the people longed for a Savior who would bring peace and restore what had been broken. When Jesus entered the world, that promise found fulfillment. The true Light had come, and the darkness could not overcome it.

We still encounter darkness in many forms: doubt, fear, suffering, and uncertainty. Yet Advent reminds us that no shadow runs too deep for God's light to reach. Every time we choose faith over fear, every time we turn to prayer instead of despair, the light of Christ shines again in our lives and in our world.

We not only receive the light of Jesus but also reflect it. As we draw near to Him, His light grows within us and becomes a beacon for others who cannot yet see the dawn. This is the hope of Advent: that even in our waiting, the light of Christ already shines, and His presence transforms the night into day.

JOURNAL PROMPTS

1. What specific "darkness" in your life - fear, grief, confusion, sin - needs the light of Christ right now? Will you invite Him into that place today?

2. Look at your daily path this week: your workplace, your neighborhood, your home. Where is one dark place (figuratively or literally) where you could shine Christ's light through a specific act of kindness, truth, or hope?

PRAYER

Lord Jesus,
You are the Light that never fades.
Shine into every dark place of my heart
and fill me with Your peace.
Let Your light guide me through uncertainty
and give me courage to walk in faith.
May Your brightness reflect through me
so that others might see Your love and find hope in You.
Father, I ask this in Jesus' name,
through the power of the Holy Spirit.
Amen.

WEEK 2

A Week to Renew the Heart

PREPARE THE WAY

The second week of Advent invites us to prepare not only our surroundings but the inner space of our hearts.

John the Baptist's call still echoes through time: "Prepare the way of the Lord, make his paths straight." Preparing for Christ's coming means making room for His presence by releasing what keeps us from Him. We clear away the distractions, burdens, and habits that crowd our spiritual lives.

True preparation begins with honesty before God. We reflect on what needs healing, forgiveness, or change. When we turn back to the Lord with sincerity, we discover that His mercy already goes before us. Repentance opens the doorway to freedom and peace. In returning to God, we find joy waiting for us.

THIS WEEK'S JOURNEY:

- o Day 8: A Voice in the Wilderness - Hearing God's call in quiet places
- o Day 9: The Gift of Repentance - Embracing the grace of turning back
- o Day 10: A Clean Heart - Receiving God's renewing work
- o Day 11: Turning Toward the Light - Choosing Christ over darkness

25

- Day 12: The Peace of Surrender - Trusting God's wisdom
- Day 13: The Courage to Change - Growing through transformation
- Day 14: A Heart That Listens - Cultivating spiritual attentiveness

PRAYER FOR THE WEEK

Lord, prepare our hearts to receive You.
Remove every obstacle that hinders our love for You.
Make us new, clean,
and ready to welcome Your presence fully.
Father, I ask this in Jesus' name,
through the power of the Holy Spirit.
Amen.

DAY 8

A VOICE IN THE WILDERNESS

"The voice of one crying out in the wilderness:
'Prepare the way of the Lord, make his paths
straight.'" Luke 3:4

DEVOTIONAL REFLECTION

When John the Baptist appeared in the wilderness, his voice shook the hearts of those who heard him.

He did not speak from the comfort of the city but from a barren place, calling people to turn their hearts back to God. In every generation, God still sends His word into the wilderness of our lives, reminding us to prepare room for His presence.

Advent calls us to listen to that voice again. It invites us to clear away the obstacles that keep us from hearing God more clearly. The wilderness moments in our lives—times of silence, loneliness, or uncertainty—become holy places where God speaks if we will listen. The Lord desires to meet us in the quiet and prepare our hearts for His coming.

Preparation begins not in our strength but in our openness. When we make space for God, He straightens the paths within us that have grown crooked or cluttered. As we respond to His call, the wilderness becomes a place of

27

encounter, and we discover that the Lord already prepares the way for us.

JOURNAL PROMPTS

1. Name three specific distractions or obstacles currently keeping you from hearing God's voice clearly. What is one practical step you could take today to minimize one of these distractions?

2. Who do you know who feels they're in a "wilderness" season right now? How could you be a voice of encouragement that helps prepare their heart to encounter Christ this week?

PRAYER

Lord,
Speak into the wilderness of my heart.
Help me to hear Your voice calling me closer to You.
Remove anything that keeps me
from knowing You more deeply.
Make straight the paths in my life
that have become twisted or distracted.
Prepare me, Lord, for the fullness of Your coming
and fill me with peace as I walk in Your way.
Father, I ask this in Jesus' name,
through the power of the Holy Spirit.
Amen.

THE GIFT OF REPENTANCE

"Repent, for the kingdom of heaven has come near." Matthew 3:2

DEVOTIONAL REFLECTION

Repentance stands as one of the greatest gifts God gives to His people.

It carries not guilt or shame, but grace, an invitation to turn from what harms us and return to the One who heals us. When John the Baptist preached repentance, he did not condemn people; instead, he called them to freedom. He prepared them to recognize and receive Jesus, the Lamb of God who takes away the sin of the world.

To repent means to realign our hearts with God's heart. We turn away from self-reliance and pride, turning toward mercy, humility, and love. In repentance, we find not rejection but restoration. God always stands ready to meet us with forgiveness and to breathe new life into what has grown weary or wounded.

This week, let repentance become a prayer, not a burden. Invite the Holy Spirit to reveal to you what needs to be surrendered and healed. As you do, you will discover again that repentance does not bring punishment but preparation.

It clears the path for joy to return and creates space for Christ to dwell more fully within you.

JOURNAL PROMPTS

1. The Holy Spirit may be gently highlighting one specific area where He invites you to turn back toward Him. What is it? What concrete step of repentance could you take today?

2. Think of someone who feels trapped by shame or past mistakes. How could you model or speak about God's mercy in a way that helps them encounter His grace this week, living as an IMPACTER of restoration?

PRAYER

Merciful Father,
Thank You for the grace of repentance.
Turn my heart toward You
and away from all that keeps me distant from Your love.
Wash me clean
and renew my spirit with Your peace.
Help me to see repentance
as a gift that draws me closer to You each day.
Prepare me, Lord, to welcome Your presence
with a heart made new.
Father, I ask this in Jesus' name,
through the power of the Holy Spirit.
Amen.

DAY 10

A CLEAN HEART

"Create in me a clean heart, O God, and put a new and right spirit within me." Psalm 51:10

DEVOTIONAL REFLECTION

Every true preparation for Christ begins within.

We may decorate our homes and plan our celebrations, but God is most concerned with the condition of our hearts. King David's prayer captures what Advent preparation truly means: a plea for renewal from the inside out. When we ask God to create a clean heart in us, we open the door for His grace to heal, reshape, and restore our inner life.

Sometimes we try to fix ourselves through effort or discipline alone, yet transformation begins only when we allow God to do what we cannot. We cannot earn a clean heart; we receive it as a gift from a loving Father who delights in making us whole again. Advent invites us to release old burdens, past regrets, and lingering guilt, so that new life may grow.

When God cleanses our hearts, He also gives us a new spirit —one that is humble, courageous, and filled with peace. Each day we pray this simple prayer, we prepare the way for Christ to dwell more deeply within us. Let that be your offering today: an open heart and a willing spirit.

31

JOURNAL PROMPTS

1. What specific burden, regret, or guilt have you been carrying that you need to release to God today? Write it down, then pray David's prayer over it.

2. Who in your circle carries visible shame or feels "unclean" in some way? What tangible expression of acceptance, forgiveness, or grace could you offer them this week as an IMPACTER of renewal?

PRAYER

Create in me, O God,
a heart that is pure and ready for You.
Wash away the dust and weariness that cling to my soul.
Renew my spirit with Your love
so that I may walk in truth and peace.
Help me to forgive where I need to forgive,
to surrender what I cannot control,
and to welcome Your transforming grace.
Make my heart a home for You this Advent.
Father, I ask this in Jesus' name,
through the power of the Holy Spirit.
Amen.

DAY 11

TURNING TOWARD THE LIGHT

"For once you were darkness, but now in the Lord
you are light. Live as children of light."
Ephesians 5:8

DEVOTIONAL REFLECTION

When Christ comes into a person's life, everything begins to change.

The shadows of confusion and sin give way to the brightness of His truth. Paul reminds us that we were once in darkness, but now we are light in the Lord. This transformation is not our own doing; it flows from God's grace. Advent calls us to remember that transformation and to prepare for His coming by actively turning toward the light.

Preparing for Jesus requires more than clearing away what is wrong; it means actively turning our whole being toward Him. Repentance, at its heart, is a turning away from darkness and toward light, away from self and toward God. Every act of kindness, every word of forgiveness, every moment of prayer steps us closer to the Light. Christ's light not only shines upon us but also through us, making us bearers of His presence in the world.

33

As you turn toward Christ, you become part of His light in the darkness. Your faith, your joy and your love matter immensely. They are Christ's very presence shining in a world that desperately needs to see that the Light has come and the darkness will not overcome it.

JOURNAL PROMPTS

1. What specific area of your life - a relationship, a habit, a thought pattern - remains in shadow and needs the light of Christ during this Advent season? Will you turn it toward Him today?

2. Your daily path crosses people walking in various kinds of darkness. Who specifically comes to mind? How could you reflect Christ's light to them this week through word or deed, becoming an IMPACTER of joy and truth?

PRAYER

Lord Jesus,
You are the Light that guides my steps
and warms my heart.
Turn me fully toward You
so that I may walk in Your truth.
Remove any darkness
that clouds my thoughts or actions.
Let Your light shine through me
so that others might find hope in You.
Father, I ask this in Jesus' name,
through the power of the Holy Spirit.
Amen.

DAY 12

THE PEACE OF SURRENDER

"Trust in the Lord with all your heart, and do not rely on your own insight. In all your ways acknowledge him, and he will make straight your paths." Proverbs 3:5-6

DEVOTIONAL REFLECTION

One of the greatest ways to prepare for the Lord is to surrender our need to control.

We cling tightly to our plans, our understanding, and our timing, hoping that everything will unfold as we imagine. Yet Advent reminds us that God's plans always rise higher and reach further than our own. When we trust Him fully, our hearts rest and our paths become clear.

Surrender is not weakness; it is faith in motion. It becomes a quiet decision to believe that God knows what is best, even when we cannot see the full picture. Mary, the mother of Jesus, lived this kind of surrender when she said, *"Let it be done to me according to your word."* Her yes to God changed history, and it began with simple trust.

When we lay down our anxieties and acknowledge God in every part of our lives, He straightens the paths that seemed tangled or uncertain. Peace flows where we once strove. Today, as you prepare your heart for Christ, let surrender

35

become your prayer. The God who came for you proves trustworthy, and He will never lead you astray.

JOURNAL PROMPTS

1. What is the one area of your life you find most challenging to surrender to God's care right now? Be honest about what makes it difficult. What fear underlies your need to control it?

2. Who do you know who is exhausted from trying to control everything? What testimony of God's faithfulness in your own surrender could you share with them this week as an IMPACTER of peace?

PRAYER

Lord,
I place my trust in You.
Teach me to surrender every plan
and every worry into Your loving hands.
When I cannot see the way forward,
help me to rest in Your wisdom.
Straighten the paths before me
and fill my heart with peace.
Let my surrender become a sign of faith
that prepares the way for You to come
more fully into my life.
Father, I ask this in Jesus' name,
through the power of the Holy Spirit.
Amen.

DAY 13

THE COURAGE TO CHANGE

"Do not be conformed to this world, but be transformed by the renewing of your minds, so that you may discern what is the will of God, what is good and acceptable and perfect." Romans 12:2

DEVOTIONAL REFLECTION

Preparing for the Lord's coming always requires change.

Advent invites us to look honestly at our lives and ask where God might be calling us to grow. Change can feel uncomfortable, even frightening, but it opens the path to transformation. The Apostle Paul reminds us that renewal starts in the mind, in the way we think, perceive, and understand what God desires for us.

God's Spirit gently shapes us when we allow Him to renew our thoughts and attitudes. The patterns of the world often pull us toward fear, comparison, and self-focus, but the Spirit draws us toward love, humility, and peace. Transformation concerns not perfection but becoming new each day as we learn to live in God's will.

When we courageously change, we create room for new life. Each time we release an old habit, forgive a wound, or choose kindness over judgment, the way of the Lord becomes clearer within us. Advent change brings not

37

burdens but blessings; God prepares the heart for greater joy.

JOURNAL PROMPTS

1. If God's Spirit could change one thing about your thought patterns, attitudes, or habits this Advent, what would it be? What is one small, concrete step you could take toward that change this week?

2. Change requires courage, and everyone needs encouragement. Who in your life is attempting a difficult change or transformation? How could you support them practically this week, becoming an IMPACTER of renewal and hope?

PRAYER

Lord,
Give me the courage to change
where You are calling me to grow.
Renew my mind with Your truth
and fill me with the strength of Your Spirit.
Free me from the patterns of this world
that keep me from Your peace.
Teach me to see as You see,
to think as You think,
and to love as You love.
Let my life be transformed by Your grace.
Father, I ask this in Jesus' name,
through the power of the Holy Spirit.
Amen.

DAY 14

A HEART THAT LISTENS

Speak, Lord, for your servant is listening."
1 Samuel 3:9

DEVOTIONAL REFLECTION

When the young Samuel first heard God's voice, he did not recognize it.

It took quietness, guidance, and willingness to respond before he learned to say, *"Speak, Lord, for your servant is listening."* Advent calls us to cultivate that same posture of the heart to listen more deeply for the gentle voice of God that speaks in prayer, in Scripture, through the wisdom of the Church and in the stillness of our days.

Listening means more than hearing; we open ourselves to respond. God always speaks, but His voice reaches best those willing to obey. A listening heart creates space for transformation. When we pause long enough to hear Him, we often find that His words bring direction, peace, and renewal.

In a noisy world filled with constant distractions, taking time to listen becomes an act of faith. As you move through this Advent season, allow moments of silence to become encounters with God. He still speaks to the humble and

39

attentive heart. When you listen, you will find that He not only speaks to you, He speaks within you.

JOURNAL PROMPTS

1. When was the last time I truly paused to listen for God's voice in my life?

2. How can I model a listening heart for others and become an IMPACTER of discernment and peace in my relationships?

PRAYER

Lord,
Quiet my heart so that I may hear Your voice.
Teach me to listen with faith
and to respond with love.
In the busyness of my days,
help me to make space for Your presence.
Let Your words shape my choices and guide my steps.
May I live with a listening heart
that is always ready to follow where You lead.
Father, I ask this in Jesus' name,
through the power of the Holy Spirit.
Amen.

WEEK 3

A Week to Rejoice in His Presence

REJOICE, HE IS NEAR

The third week of Advent shines with joy.

The waiting no longer weighs heavy with longing but brightens with the promise that the Lord draws near. The rose-colored candle on the Advent wreath reminds us to rejoice, not because all seems perfect, but because God keeps faith and His presence already dwells among us. We do not find joy in circumstances; we find it in Christ's nearness as He comes to dwell with His people.

This week invites us to open our eyes and hearts to signs of His presence in everyday life. We see Him in quiet acts of love, in moments of prayer, in the beauty of creation, and in the warmth of community. When we choose gratitude over complaint and trust over fear, joy rises within us like morning light.

Advent joy endures deeply. It does not deny pain or difficulty but reminds us that we do not face them alone. Christ has entered our world, and His joy strengthens us. As we draw closer to Christmas, let our hearts echo Mary's song: *"My soul magnifies the Lord, and my spirit rejoices in God my Savior."*

THIS WEEK'S JOURNEY

- Day 15: The Path of Peace - Walking in God's shalom
- Day 16: The Joy of His Nearness - Finding confidence in God's presence
- Day 17: Joy in the Ordinary - Discovering Christ in daily life
- Day 18: The Joy of Giving - Reflecting God's generosity
- Day 19: Joy That Strengthens - Drawing power from God's presence
- Day 20: Joy in Believing - Trusting while we wait
- Day 21: Emmanuel, God With Us - Celebrating the promise fulfilled

PRAYER FOR THE WEEK

Lord of joy, fill our hearts with the gladness
that comes from knowing You are near.
Help us see Your presence in all things
and to share that joy with a world
that desperately needs it.
Father, I ask this in Jesus' name,
through the power of the Holy Spirit.
Amen.

DAY 15

THE PATH OF PEACE

---

*"By the tender mercy of our God, the dawn from
on high will break upon us, to give light to those
who sit in darkness and in the shadow of death, to
guide our feet into the way of peace." Luke 1:78-79*

DEVOTIONAL REFLECTION

When the dawn of Christ breaks into our lives, peace
follows.

Zechariah's song overflows with joy at the mercy of God,
who comes to bring light to those who sit in darkness. This
is what Advent joy looks like. It is not loud or fleeting, but
steady and full of promise. It quietly assures us that the
Lord Himself has drawn near to guide our feet into the way
of peace.

But what is this "way of peace"? It is not merely the absence
of conflict, but a path we walk - a journey of following
Christ.

Peace and joy walk together on the journey of faith. Both
flow from Christ's presence. His peace does not mean the
absence of struggle, but the calm assurance that we are
never alone. His joy steadies our hearts and reminds us that
even when life feels uncertain, His light already shines ahead
of us, showing us the next step.

HE IS COMING ADVENT DEVOTIONAL

As you walk through this day, let Christ's peace be your pathway and His joy your strength. In His light, there is hope, peace, and joy for all who believe.

JOURNAL PROMPTS

1. Think about your typical day, your commute, your work, your evening routine. Where specifically are you walking in anxiety rather than peace? What would it look like to let Christ guide your feet into His shalom in that situation?

2. The "way of peace" is not just personal but communal. Where is there broken peace in your family, workplace, or church? What concrete step toward reconciliation, harmony, or wholeness could you take this week as an IMPACTER of peace?

PRAYER

Lord Jesus,
Thank You for guiding my heart into the path of peace.
Fill me with joy that comes from knowing You are near.
When anxiety or fear rises,
remind me that Your light
has already broken through the darkness.
Help me to walk in peace
and harmony with You and others.
Let me carry Your peace wherever I go.
Father, I ask this in Jesus' name,
through the power of the Holy Spirit. Amen.

DAY 16

THE JOY OF HIS NEARNESS

"The Lord is near. Do not worry about anything, but in everything by prayer and supplication with thanksgiving let your requests be made known to God." Philippians 4:5-6

DEVOTIONAL REFLECTION

The Lord is near.

Four words that change everything. Advent joy does not come loud or fleeting; it arrives as quiet confidence in God's nearness. Paul's words remind us that joy begins where anxiety ends in the awareness that the Lord stands close. When we believe that, our hearts can rest. Joy takes root when trust replaces worry and gratitude becomes our prayer.

Christ's presence transforms everything. We may still face challenges, but His nearness brings peace to places where fear once lived. When we turn our worries into prayer, our hearts begin to lighten, and joy grows stronger. This joy depends not on what we have but on who walks with us. The Lord does not stand far away; He comes close enough to hear every prayer and hold every tear.

Paul connects the Lord's nearness directly to our prayer life. Notice the progression: because the Lord is near, we need

45

not worry; instead, we pray with thanksgiving. Nearness invites intimacy. And in that conversation, joy flows.

As you journey through this week, let your joy come from the simple assurance that Jesus draws near. Whisper His name often. Pause to notice His presence. Allow His peace to fill your heart. Joy will follow, not as a feeling to chase but as a gift that flows from knowing Him.

JOURNAL PROMPTS

1. The Lord is near, but where do you most need to feel His nearness right now? In what specific situation this week do you need to remember "He is close enough to hear"?

2. Joy becomes contagious when we share it with others. Who in your life needs the encouragement that God is near to them? Write them a note, send them a message, or tell them in person this week.

PRAYER

Lord Jesus,
You are near to those who call upon Your name.
Calm my anxious thoughts and fill my heart with gratitude.
Teach me to bring every concern
to You in prayer and to trust in Your loving care.
Let Your nearness become my source of joy today.
May I carry Your peace wherever I go.
Father, I ask this in Jesus' name,
through the power of the Holy Spirit. Amen.

DAY 17

JOY IN THE ORDINARY

"Rejoice in the Lord always; again I will say, Rejoice." Philippians 4:4

DEVOTIONAL REFLECTION

Joy often comes quietly, hidden in the ordinary rhythm of life.

We look for it in big moments, yet God places it in the small ones - a kind word, a sunrise, a moment of peace that reminds us He draws near. God is with you exactly where you are. You don't have to go somewhere else to find Him; He meets you in the midst of your day, in the places that seem most familiar.

The joy Paul speaks of differs from surface happiness. It offers steady assurance that God is present and working, even when life feels uncertain. Joy grows when gratitude replaces complaint and when faith looks beyond what is visible. It quietly assures us that the Lord's nearness is stronger than any worry.

This Advent, look for Jesus in the simple, unnoticed places through conversation, prayer, and the beauty of everyday life. Rejoicing does not mean pretending everything is perfect; it means remembering that Christ walks with you in all things. When you open your eyes to His presence, even the ordinary turns holy, and joy becomes a way of life.

JOURNAL PROMPTS

1. Look back at yesterday. Where did you experience God's quiet joy in ordinary moments that you might have missed at the time? Can you name three?

2. Today, practice "joy reconnaissance" - actively look for God's presence in your routine. At the end of the day, record what you found. Then share one of these discoveries with someone, becoming an IMPACTER of attentiveness and hope.

PRAYER

Lord Jesus,
Help me to find joy
in the ordinary moments of this day.
Open my heart to see Your presence
in the simple and familiar.
When life feels routine or weary,
remind me that You are near
and that Your joy gives me strength.
Fill me with gratitude
and let my life reflect Your peace to others.
Father, I ask this in Jesus' name,
through the power of the Holy Spirit.
Amen.

DAY 18

THE JOY OF GIVING

"It is more blessed to give than to receive."
Acts 20:35

DEVOTIONAL REFLECTION

A unique joy comes from giving.

In Advent, we often think about gifts - what to buy, how to wrap them, and what to share. Yet the deepest joy does not flow from what we receive. It springs from the giving of ourselves. When we give from the heart, we join God in His generosity, because His very nature is to give. Every breath we take, every new day, every promise fulfilled in Christ, all express His giving love.

Giving concerns not what we have but how we love. Some of the greatest gifts are simple: forgiveness, patience, encouragement, or time. These gifts often cost us more than anything we could buy, but they carry the fragrance of heaven. When we give freely, joy grows. The act of giving draws us closer to God's heart, who gave His only Son so that we might have life.

Paul's words to the Ephesian elders remind us that Jesus Himself taught this principle. The Incarnation is the ultimate act of giving - God giving Himself to us. When we give, we reflect that divine generosity. We become like Christ. And there is deep, lasting joy in that resemblance.

As you move through this Advent week, ask the Lord to show you where and how you can give. Let your generosity reflect His love in you. When giving becomes an act of worship, your joy will not depend on circumstance but will flow from the presence of the One who gives without end.

JOURNAL PROMPTS

1. What opportunities do you have this week to give of yourself—your time, attention, resources, forgiveness, or encouragement? Choose one specific act of giving and commit to it today.
2. The joy of giving multiplies when we give without seeking recognition. What is one anonymous or secret act of generosity you could perform this week, using your resources to impact others as a quiet IMPACTER of joy?

PRAYER

Loving God,
Thank You for being the giver of every good gift.
Teach me to give with a joyful heart,
without hesitation or expectation.
Help me to see the needs around me
and respond with love and compassion.
May my generosity bring hope to others
and draw them closer to You.
Let giving become my joy and my worship this Advent.
Father, I ask this in Jesus' name,
through the power of the Holy Spirit. Amen.

DAY 19

JOY THAT STRENGTHENS

"You show me the path of life. In your presence there is fullness of joy; in your right hand are pleasures forevermore." Psalm 16:11

DEVOTIONAL REFLECTION

Joy is the steady strength that grows from living in God's presence.

It differs from shallow happiness that fades with circumstance. This joy offers deep assurance that comes from knowing who holds your life. When we rest in the presence of God, His joy becomes our refuge, a quiet confidence that no challenge can steal.

Much of Advent reminds us that God does not stand far off. When we walk closely with Him, He shows us the path of life. Joy becomes a guide that keeps our hearts lifted, even in the midst of difficulty, reminding us that the Lord's hand remains steady and His promises stand sure.

Notice David's words: *"in your right hand are pleasures forevermore."* This is not a fleeting pleasure but a lasting delight that comes from being held by God. The right hand symbolizes strength, authority, and blessing. To be in God's right hand is to be secure, honored, and filled with eternal joy. This Advent, remember that God holds you there.

51

As you move through this day, seek His presence more than solutions. Joy comes from the heart that abides in Him. Let that joy strengthen you, lift you, and carry you through whatever lies ahead.

JOURNAL PROMPTS

1. When do you feel most aware of God's presence? What activities, places, or practices help you "abide" in Him? How could you build more of these into your daily rhythm?

2. Strength-giving joy is contagious. Who needs to be strengthened right now—perhaps someone facing difficulty, illness, or discouragement? How could you share joy with them this week through presence, prayer, or encouragement?

PRAYER

Lord,
Fill me with the joy
that comes from Your presence alone.
When I grow tired or discouraged,
draw me close to You and renew my strength.
Teach me to live with a heart anchored in Your love.
May Your joy become my refuge,
and may it overflow to strengthen others
who need hope today.
Father, I ask this in Jesus' name,
through the power of the Holy Spirit. Amen.

DAY 20

JOY IN BELIEVING

"May the God of hope fill you with all joy and peace in believing, so that you may abound in hope by the power of the Holy Spirit." Romans 15:13

DEVOTIONAL REFLECTION

Faith and joy connect deeply.

Joy flows from trust, the quiet confidence that God will do what He has promised. Paul prays that the God of hope would fill us with joy and peace in believing. Notice the timing: not only when everything works out, but while we are still believing, still waiting, still trusting. Joy begins to rise within us even before we see the answer.

Advent is a season of believing in what we cannot yet see. Each candle we light, each prayer we whisper, becomes an act of faith that God's promises unfold even now. When our faith leans on His goodness rather than our understanding, the Holy Spirit fills us with joy that no circumstance can take away. This is the joy that sustains the waiting heart.

Paul's prayer reveals a beautiful cycle: believing leads to joy and peace, which lead to abounding hope, all through the power of the Holy Spirit. This is not willpower or positive

53

thinking. This is the Spirit's work in us. When we choose to believe, we open ourselves to receive His joy.

Today, choose to believe again, not because you can see the outcome, but because you know the One who holds it. As faith grows, joy follows. The more we trust in His love, the more our lives become signs of His presence in the world.

JOURNAL PROMPTS

1. What specific promise of God do you struggle to believe right now? Write it down. Then write beneath it: "I choose to believe..." How does choosing belief change your perspective?

2. Faith-filled joy witnesses powerfully to others. Who in your life needs to see an example of joy rooted in belief rather than circumstance? How could you share your journey of trusting God with them today?

PRAYER

God of hope,
Fill me with joy and peace
as I believe in Your promises.
Strengthen my faith when doubts arise
and help me to rest in Your unfailing love.
Let the Holy Spirit fill me with joy
that overflows into every part of my life.
May my trust in You become a light
that points others to Your goodness.
Father, I ask this in Jesus' name,
through the power of the Holy Spirit. Amen.

DAY 21

EMMANUEL, GOD WITH US

"Look, the virgin shall conceive and bear a son,
and they shall name him Emmanuel," which
means, "God is with us."
Matthew 1:23

DEVOTIONAL REFLECTION

One word contains the heart of the Christmas story:
Emmanuel.

God is with us. He does not stand distant, not watching
from afar, but dwelling in the very midst of our lives. In
Jesus, the invisible God becomes visible, entering our world
with compassion and love.

God's presence changes how we see everything. We no
longer face challenges alone, for He walks beside us. We no
longer carry the weight of our burdens by ourselves,
because He walks with us in every joy and in every struggle.
Emmanuel means that wherever you are, God is there too,
in your home, in your work, in your silence, and in your
prayer.

This is different from merely knowing God is near (Day 16).
Emmanuel declares that God has come to stay. He has not
just drawn close for a visit; He has moved in. The
Incarnation is permanent; God is forever united with

55

humanity. And through His Spirit, He makes His home in us. This is intimacy beyond proximity. This is family. This is love that will never leave.

Take a moment today to rest in that truth. Let the reality of Emmanuel bring peace to your heart and confidence to your steps, for you are never alone.

JOURNAL PROMPTS

1. *"God with us"* is not abstract theology but daily reality. In what specific situation this week do you most need to remember that God is with you, not just watching, but present, involved, and active?

2. Who around you feels alone, abandoned, or isolated? How could you tangibly express *"God is with you"* to them this week - through presence, not just words - becoming an IMPACTER of His incarnate love?

PRAYER

Lord Jesus,
You are Emmanuel, God with us.
Thank You for drawing near
and for dwelling in my heart.
When I feel alone or uncertain,
remind me of Your constant presence.
Fill me with peace that cannot be shaken.
Help me to live today aware of You
and to share the assurance of Your nearness with others.
Father, I ask this in Jesus' name,
through the power of the Holy Spirit. Amen.

WEEK 4

A Week to Live in His Light

HE IS HERE

The final week of Advent brings us to the edge of mystery and fulfillment.

The waiting gives way to wonder as we prepare to celebrate the coming of Emmanuel, God with us. The promise we have longed for no longer stands distant; He is here. The One we awaited enters quietly, not with fanfare but with love so great that it transforms everything.

This week calls us to live in the light of His presence. We pause and recognize that God has already drawn near to us. His presence transforms the ordinary and fills even the simplest moments with grace. The manger teaches us that holiness often comes to humble places, and that Christ's presence matters most of all.

As we approach Christmas, may our hearts overflow with gratitude. The Lord we awaited has come, and He continues to come, again and again, into our lives. May this final week renew our awe, deepen our peace, and inspire us to carry His light into the world.

THIS WEEK'S JOURNEY

- ○ Day 22: The Presence That Brings Peace - Resting in Christ's shalom

- Day 23: The Light of the World - Following Jesus' illumination
- Day 24: The Humble King - Bowing before servant majesty
- Day 25: The God Who Comes Close - Celebrating the Incarnation
- Day 26: The Night of Promise - Standing on Christmas Eve's threshold
- Christmas Day: The Light Has Come - Rejoicing in fulfillment

PRAYER FOR THE WEEK

Come, Lord Jesus. You are here.
Open our eyes to see You,
our hearts to receive You,
and our lives to reflect You.
Fill us with wonder at Your coming,
and let our joy overflow to all we meet.
Father, I ask this in Jesus' name,
through the power of the Holy Spirit. Amen

DAY 22

THE PRESENCE THAT BRINGS PEACE

"Peace I leave with you; my peace I give to you. I do not give to you as the world gives. Do not let your hearts be troubled, and do not let them be afraid." John 14:27

DEVOTIONAL REFLECTION

The peace that Jesus offers differs from anything the world can give.

It does not depend on circumstances or the absence of trouble. It flows from His presence, a peace that settles the heart even when life remains uncertain. When Jesus spoke these words to His disciples, He prepared them for change and challenge, yet He promised that His peace would remain with them always.

Today, we focus on peace as a gift Christ gives - something He possesses and bestows. This is not peace we achieve through right actions or positive thinking. This is the very peace of Christ Himself, transferred to us, like a treasure placed in our hands.

Advent reminds us that we do not chase peace; we welcome Someone. The Prince of Peace has come and continues to dwell among us.

Today, invite His peace to quiet your thoughts and steady your heart. In the middle of noise and activity, pause and remember that His peace already lies within reach.

JOURNAL PROMPTS

1. Jesus says, *"Do not let your hearts be troubled."* What specific trouble or fear is troubling your heart today? Will you accept His gift of peace for that situation right now?

2. Peace-givers change atmospheres. Where could you bring the peace of Christ this week, perhaps a tense meeting, a difficult conversation, or a chaotic environment? Plan how you'll carry His peace into that space as an IMPACTER of calm.

PRAYER

Lord Jesus,
You are my peace.
When my heart feels restless or anxious,
help me to turn to You.
Teach me to trust that
Your presence is enough to calm every fear.
Fill me with the peace that only You can give,
and let that peace flow through me
to others who need it most.
Father, I ask this in Jesus' name,
through the power of the Holy Spirit. Amen.

DAY 23

THE LIGHT OF THE WORLD

"Again, Jesus spoke to them, saying, 'I am the light of the world. Whoever follows me will never walk in darkness but will have the light of life.'"
John 8:12

DEVOTIONAL REFLECTION

Throughout every age, the world has known both light and darkness.

Jesus steps into this world and declares Himself to be the Light that no darkness can overcome. His light does not merely expose what hides; it brings healing, direction, and life. Those who follow Him walk in the steady glow of His presence, even when the path ahead seems uncertain.

Great comfort comes from knowing that we need not create our own light. Christ shines within us, guiding our steps when we cannot see ahead. The more we follow Him, the more His light fills our hearts and overflows into the lives of others. His light reminds us that love proves stronger than fear and that hope still burns in the darkest night.

John's Gospel emphasizes that Jesus is not just a light, but the light - the source of all spiritual illumination. To follow Jesus means to walk in increasing brightness, growing more alive with each step.

61

Today, open your heart to the light of Christ. As His light fills you, carry it into conversations, decisions, and small acts of kindness.

JOURNAL PROMPTS

1. Where in your life do you most need Christ's light right now to expose something hidden, to guide a decision, or to bring warmth to a cold place? Ask Him specifically to shine there today.

2. Jesus calls us to reflect His light. Look at your week ahead: where will you encounter darkness (despair, confusion, sin, oppression)? How could you intentionally bring His light there through specific words or actions, living as an IMPACTER of illumination?

PRAYER

Lord Jesus,
You are the Light of the world
and the light of my life.
Shine into every shadow of my heart
and lead me in Your truth.
When I feel lost or uncertain,
help me to follow where Your light leads.
Fill me so completely
that Your light overflows to others,
bringing hope and peace wherever I go.
Father, I ask this in Jesus' name,
through the power of the Holy Spirit.
Amen.

DAY 24

THE HUMBLE KING

"He humbled himself and became obedient to the point of death, even death on a cross." Philippians 2:8

DEVOTIONAL REFLECTION

When we picture a king, we imagine power and grandeur.

Yet the King who comes to us at Christmas arrives in humility, born in a stable, wrapped in cloth, laid in a manger. From His first breath, Jesus shows us a different kind of greatness. His humility does not diminish His majesty but reveals it. The God of heaven stoops low to meet us where we are, showing that love's strength comes through gentleness.

Christ's humility opens the doorway where we meet God. Advent invites us to mirror that same humility, to release pride, entitlement, and self-sufficiency, and to kneel before the One who knelt for us. In humility, we become open to grace, able to receive the gifts we cannot earn.

Because Christ humbled Himself, God exalted Him to the highest place. The pattern is clear: the way up is down. The path to glory runs through humility.

When we choose humility, we walk in the footsteps of the King. We begin to see others through His eyes and to serve

63

with His heart. True greatness does not seek notice but creates space for God's presence to shine through us. The humble King still reigns, and His throne establishes itself in hearts that bow before Him in love.

JOURNAL PROMPTS

1. Where is God inviting you to grow in humility this Advent? Is it in a relationship, at work, in your thought life, or in how you view yourself compared to others?

2. Humility attracts people to Christ; pride repels them. How can embracing humility make your witness stronger this week? What practical act of humble service could you offer someone, becoming an IMPACTER of Christlike love?

PRAYER

Lord Jesus,
You are the humble King
who came not to be served but to serve.
Teach me the beauty of humility
and the strength that comes from surrender.
Free me from pride
and help me to walk in love and gentleness.
May my life reflect Your heart
and make room for others to see Your glory.
Father, I ask this in Jesus' name,
through the power of the Holy Spirit.
Amen.

THE GOD WHO COMES CLOSE

---

*"And the Word became flesh and lived among us,
and we have seen his glory, the glory as of a
father's only son, full of grace and truth."* John 1:14

DEVOTIONAL REFLECTION

The wonder of Christmas comes in this: God has come close.

The eternal Word became flesh and made His home among us. In Jesus, God does not remain far away or beyond reach; He enters our world completely. He knows what it is to laugh, to weep, to work, to walk the same earth we walk. God's glory no longer hides in mystery but reveals itself in the face of Christ.

This truth transforms everything. It means that no place seems too ordinary, no heart too broken, no life too small for His presence. God comes to us as we are, not as we wish we were. He chooses to dwell in the midst of our humanity so that we might share in His divinity. Grace and truth meet in Him, and through Him we learn what love truly looks like.

As Christmas arrives, let this reality settle deep in your heart: God does not stand distant. He comes close, closer than your breath, nearer than your thoughts. The same Word

65

who became flesh still speaks peace into our lives today. Let His presence fill you with wonder and renew your faith that the light of the world has come to stay.

JOURNAL PROMPTS

1. Christmas can become so busy that we miss the wonder of the season. Today, take fifteen minutes in complete quiet. Light a candle. Reflect on the miracle: God became human for you. What does your heart want to say to Him?

2. The Incarnation means God enters human life - all of it. Where do you most need to recognize God's presence in your ordinary life today? How will you help someone else see that God comes close to them, too, living as an IMPACTER of wonder?

PRAYER

Lord Jesus,
You are the Word made flesh,
the God who comes close.
Thank You for entering our world
and walking among us.
Help me to recognize Your presence in my life
and to carry Your grace and truth into every situation.
Fill my heart with awe
at the mystery of Your love.
May Your closeness be my comfort and my strength.
Father, I ask this in Jesus' name,
through the power of the Holy Spirit.
Amen.

THE NIGHT OF PROMISE

---

*"But the angel said to them, 'Do not be afraid; for
see, I am bringing you good news of great joy for all
the people: to you is born this day in the city of
David a Savior, who is the Messiah, the Lord.'"*
Luke 2:10-11

DEVOTIONAL REFLECTION

The night fell quietly over Bethlehem, yet heaven refused to
stay silent.

Angels filled the sky with light and song, proclaiming the
greatest news the world had ever heard: a Savior has been
born. In that moment, everything changed. The waiting
ended, the promise found fulfillment, and hope took on
flesh and blood. Jesus, the Messiah, had come.

Christmas Eve invites us to pause in wonder at this holy
mystery. God's plan, long spoken by the prophets, unfolds
in the stillness of night. The Savior of the world comes not
to a palace but to a stable, not to the powerful but to those
humble enough to listen. The same God who stepped into
the darkness of that night still enters the quiet corners of
our lives to bring light and peace.

As we stand on the threshold of Christmas, let your heart
rejoice. The good news is for everyone - for you, for your

family, and for the world. Do not be afraid. Lift your eyes to the light that has come and let joy fill your soul. The Savior comes, and His love will never end.

JOURNAL PROMPTS

1. On this holy night, what fears do you need to release as you hear the angel's words: *"Do not be afraid"*? Name them and leave them at the manger.

2. The shepherds heard the good news and immediately went to see it and then to share it. Tomorrow, when you gather with family or friends, how will you be intentional about sharing the good news of Christ's coming as an IMPACTER of joy?

PRAYER

Lord Jesus,
On this holy night, I thank You
for the gift of Your coming.
Fill my heart with wonder and gratitude
as I remember the beauty of Your birth.
Let Your peace rest on my home
and on all who wait for You in faith.
Help me carry the joy of this night
into every day of my life.
You are my Savior and my hope, now and forever.
Father, I ask this in Jesus' name,
through the power of the Holy Spirit.
Amen.

CHRISTMAS DAY

THE LIGHT HAS COME

"The people who walked in darkness have seen a great light; those who lived in a land of deep darkness, on them light has shined." Isaiah 9:2

DEVOTIONAL REFLECTION

Today, the waiting ends.

The long nights of anticipation give way to the brilliance of morning. The Light has come, and His name is Jesus. The child born in Bethlehem is the Savior who brings heaven to earth and fills our hearts with peace. What was promised now finds fulfillment; God's love has taken on flesh and lives among us.

Christmas celebrates not only what happened once long ago; it reminds us that Christ still comes to us. He enters every moment of joy and every place of need, every prayer whispered in faith, and every act of love given in His name. His light still shines in our world, and no darkness can overcome it.

Isaiah's prophecy, spoken 700 years before the birth of Christ, has been fulfilled. The people who walked in darkness and that includes all of us, have seen a great light. Not a flicker, not a dim glow, but a great light. This light exposes, yes, but more importantly, it illuminates, warms, guides, and gives life. This is the light we celebrate today.

Let your heart rejoice today. The Savior has come, not just for the world, but for you. As you celebrate this holy day, receive His peace and carry His light wherever you go.

JOURNAL PROMPTS

1. Christmas Day arrives! How is your heart different today than it was on Day 1 of this Advent journey? What has God shown you or changed in you over these past weeks?
2. The Light has come—now what? As you move beyond Advent into the rest of the year, what one practice from this devotional will you continue? How will you continue to live as an IMPACTER of hope in the world?

PRAYER

Lord Jesus,
Thank You for the gift of Your coming.
You are the Light that no darkness can overcome.
Fill my heart with the joy of Your presence
and the peace of knowing that I am loved.
Let this Christmas renew my faith
and awaken my desire to live for You each day.
Shine through me so that others may see Your glory
and know that You are near.
Father, I ask this in Jesus' name,
through the power of the Holy Spirit.
Amen.

WHAT'S NEXT?

The journey of Advent continues beyond the manger; it starts there.

Christmas brings the moment when heaven and earth meet, and the light of Christ takes up residence within us. The One we awaited has come, and now He calls us to carry His presence into the world. We no longer merely receive grace; we bear it into every corner of our lives.

LIVING AS AN IMPACTER

Throughout this devotional, you've reflected on what it means to be an IMPACTER, someone transformed by Christ and sent to reflect His transformation to the world. This calling does not require grand gestures. It happens when His love shapes our words, our choices, and our relationships. We reflect the light we've received: in kindness offered to the weary, in forgiveness extended to the broken, in hope spoken to those who cannot yet see the dawn. Every small act of faith joins God's great work of renewal.

As this Advent journey comes to a close, a new one begins. Christ is here. His Spirit lives within you. Let your life testify that the Savior has come. Wherever you go, carry the joy, peace, and light He has given you.

A DAILY PRAYER FOR THE JOURNEY AHEAD

Let this prayer guide you as you continue walking with Christ:

> Come, Lord Jesus, live in me,
> shine through me,
> and use my life to impact the world for You.

CONTINUING THE RHYTHMS OF ADVENT

The practices you've developed over **these** twenty-six days - daily Scripture reading, reflective prayer, journaling, and spiritual attentiveness - need not end with the season. Consider how you might continue:

Daily Time in Scripture and Prayer

Continue the habit of daily time with God. The rhythm you've established during Advent can carry you through the entire year. If you seek guidance for continued spiritual growth, numerous resources are available to help you maintain a vital connection with the Lord.

Gather with Others

Faith flourishes in community. If you have journeyed through this devotional alone, consider inviting others to join you in future spiritual practices. Whether through a small group, a prayer partner, or online fellowship, we grow stronger together. We were created for connection with God and with one another.

Live Your Faith in the Everyday

Discipleship happens not just in quiet moments of prayer but also in the ordinary rhythms of daily life at home, at work and in your neighborhood. Let the lessons you've learned through Advent inspire your words, actions, and relationships. Be the hands, feet, and heart of Jesus in your daily world. Look for the ordinary moments that become opportunities to be IMPACTER, reflecting His extraordinary love.

Walk with Support and Encouragement

The Christian life was never meant to be walked alone. Bruce Downes Ministries exists to support believers like you in growing deeper in faith and living more fully for Christ. Through daily devotionals, teaching, and community connections, we are here to walk alongside you. If you would like to stay connected and continue receiving encouragement for your faith journey, we would love to have you join our community.

Your partnership - through prayer, participation, or support - enables this ministry to reach more people around the world with the message of hope and transformation in Christ. If God has used this devotional in your life, prayerfully consider how you might help others encounter that same hope.

AS YOU GO

As you move forward, remember that you are not alone. The Lord who came to you in this Advent season walks with you every day. He is faithful. He is near. And He will complete the good work He has begun in you.

May you continue to grow in faith, be strengthened by His love, and walk boldly in the light of His presence. Keep seeking, keep trusting, and keep walking with God.

The waiting has ended, but the wonder never will.

Grace and peace to you from God our Father and the Lord Jesus Christ.

Bruce Downes
The Catholic Guy Ministry

Daily Devotionals

How to Pray with Holy Spirit Power

Learn to pray with boldness and intimacy as this devotional equips you to partner with the Holy Spirit in your everyday conversations with God.

Lent

Journey through Lent with inspiring daily reflections that draw you closer to God through prayer, Scripture, and spiritual renewal.

Resurrection Living

Step into the power of the risen Christ with 30 days of reflections that awaken hope, deepen faith, and lead you into a transformed life.

The Holy Spirit Powered Life

Discover how to live each day with strength, clarity, and purpose by allowing the Holy Spirit to guide, shape, and empower your life.

For these books and more visit: **BruceDownes.org/Store**

Prayer

Personal Prayer

This inspiring prayer book invites you to encounter the Holy Spirit in a deeper way—renewing your heart, guiding your life, and transforming your relationship with God.

Come Holy Spirit

A powerful collection of prayers and reflections inviting the Holy Spirit to renew your heart, guide your life, and transform your relationship with God.

Pray for Someone You Love

A helpful guide to interceding for those you care about, with powerful prayers and encouragement to trust God for transformation in the lives of your loved ones.

Prayers to the Holy Spirit

This prayer book will lead you into a deeper relationship with God by inviting the Holy Spirit to transform your life with power, peace, and purpose each day.

For these books and more visit: **BruceDownes.org/Store**

Spiritual Growth

7 Life changing Habits you can Learn from Mary

Discover the power of surrender, strength, and spiritual growth through seven transformative habits inspired by the life of Mary, the mother of Jesus.

Radical Forgiveness

This powerful book invites you to break free from the pain of the past and experience the life-changing freedom that only comes through God's radical gift of forgiveness.

Start Strong

This empowering book will help you gain clarity, rebuild confidence, and start strong as you pursue the life God created you to live.

90 Days of Renewal

Experience lasting spiritual transformation with this 90-day journey of prayer, reflection, and life-changing habits to renew your relationship with God.

For these books and more visit: **BruceDownes.org/Store**

Unshakeable Determination

This inspiring book will help you trust God in every season of life, overcome obstacles, and live with purpose by setting your heart firmly on who He's calling you to be.

Begin Again

No matter where you are or what you've been through, this powerful book will help you find the faith, courage, and practical steps to begin again and live the life God has planned for you.

Fighting for Your Promised Land

Discover how to boldly pursue the life God has planned for you by trusting His promises, overcoming obstacles, and stepping into your personal Promised Land.

Overcoming Your Giants

Inspired by the story of David, this book equips you with faith-filled strategies to overcome life's toughest challenges and step into the future God has planned for you.

Walking in Faith

This powerful book reveals how living by faith unlocks God's blessing, mercy, and power, even when life feels uncertain or overwhelming.